# Transition Movement for Churches

# Transition Movement for Churches

Tim Gorringe
and
Rosie Beckham

CANTERBURY PRESS

Norwich

© Tim Gorringe and Rosie Beckham 2013

First published in 2013 by the Canterbury Press Norwich
Editorial office
3rd Floor, Invicta House,
108–114 Golden Lane,
London EC1Y 0TG

Canterbury Press is an imprint of Hymns Ancient & Modern Ltd
(a registered charity)
13A Hellesdon Park Road, Norwich,
Norfolk, NR6 5DR, UK

www.canterburypress.co.uk

Scripture quotations are from the Revised Standard Version of
the Bible, copyright 1946, 1952 and 1971 by the Division of
Christian Education of the National Council of the Church of
Christ in the USA. Used by permission. All rights reserved.

British Library Cataloguing in Publication data

A catalogue record for this book is available
from the British Library


978 1 84825 507 4


Typeset by Regent Typesetting, London
Printed and bound in Great Britain by
Berforts Information Press Ltd.

# Contents

# Foreword

This book is one of the outcomes of a two-year Arts and Humanities Research Council-funded research project on 'the values which support constructive social change'. We are grateful to the Research Council, as to our local Transition groups – Exeter, Ottery St Mary and Crediton – for their help in the project. Readers familiar with Ton Veerkamp's work will recognize how indebted we are to him, and we gladly acknowledge that.

Tim Gorringe
Rosie Beckham

# List of Illustrations

The publisher and authors acknowledge with thanks permission to use copyright owners' photographs. Every effort has been made to contact the sources of photographs and we would be grateful to be informed of any omissions. Wikimedia Commons images are used by a Creative Commons Attribution-ShareAlike 3.0 licence.

# I

# Transition Towns

The slogan of the World Social Forum for the past decade has been 'Another World is Possible'. The Indian novelist Arundhati Roy says of this, 'Not only is it possible, I can already hear it growing ...'[1]

The World Social Forum networks the movements of almost 1,500 people and NGOs from around the world. It represents the hopes, aspirations and protests of what anthropologist David Graeber calls 'the 99%'. The Transition Town Movement is part of this great movement for hope and change, which seeks to articulate and realize another vision of the world than that proposed by the World Bank, the IMF, the great corporations, and most governments.

The Transition Town Movement now has nearly 400 initiatives in Britain and more than 900 worldwide, based in cities, towns and villages in 34 countries including the United States, Australasia and Japan. All over the world Transition groups are organizing practical projects to grow food, start renewable energy projects, build local homes, and re-think local economies. Examples are the

1 Arundhati Roy, 'Not Again', *The Guardian*, 30.9.2002.

Community Energy project in Lewes, East Sussex, which has covered the roof of the local brewery with photo voltaics (Solar PV), and will plough back profits into more renewable energy; and the Bath and West Community Energy group, which has done the same to local schools and is raising £5 million for more projects. Among groups working on food is a Community Supported Agriculture project in Norwich, growing food locally for local people; and the community-owned local food shop in Slaithwaite, West Yorkshire, which aims to 'declare independence from the global food system'. And in terms of the economy, there is the introduction of local currencies in Brixton, London and Bristol, which helps keep cash in the local economy, instead of leaching out to the big corporations, to be invested in tax havens.

The Transition story started in Kinsale in Ireland, when Rob Hopkins, a permaculture teacher, showed his students a film called 'The End of Suburbia', which queries the sustainability of North American suburban, car-based living, given predictions (rehearsed in detail in the film) about the likely end of cheap and easily available oil. In the 1950s North America was self-sufficient in oil, but to the incredulity of many, an oil geologist called M. King Hubbert predicted that the oil would run out by the early 1970s. His predictions were spot on – the United States now produces only 2 per cent of its own oil. He and other oil geologists then predicted that this would happen to other major oil fields in due course, and there is currently a lively debate on whether oil has already 'peaked' or whether vast resources still remain, perhaps in the Arctic. The government of George W. Bush took this sufficiently seriously to mandate that 40 per cent of the US maize crop should be processed for fuel, while in Canada it has been economically viable to produce oil from tar sands (naturally occurring bitumen deposits), although it is an immensely costly and ecologically damaging process.

The problem is that contemporary civilization is completely dependent on oil, especially for food, and as economies like China and India develop, the demand for oil will continue to rocket. If China continues developing at its present rate, it is calculated that by 2020 it alone will use the equivalent of current worldwide annual consumption.

The implications are considerable. Most of us rely on cars or buses. Many of us commute. How would we work if we could not take oil for granted? What work would we do, and how would it be organized?

The implications for food are more serious still because oil is used at virtually every level of food production, from machinery to fertilizers, from processing to delivery. Could we feed 7 billion people, or 9 billion, as is predicted for 2050, without present levels of oil? At present all but 3 per cent of the food we eat in the global North is dependent on oil.

Similarly, oil is used in the production of almost everything we use in the home and now take for granted, such as mobile phones, computers and so forth, and this is even more true for hospitals and medicine. As soon as we start asking the questions we realize that oil depletion is a threat to our way of life.

In Kinsale, Rob Hopkins asked his students to draw up an 'Energy Descent Plan' which would map out how the town would manage to feed itself, and what work it would do, post peak-oil. Together, they began to envision the transition from a world in which oil-based energy was seemingly inexhaustible to one where other resources would have to take the lead. When their work was complete they held an open meeting called 'Kinsale in 2021: Towards a Prosperous, Sustainable Future Together'. Lots of practical information was provided to show people that a series of small steps would allow them to re-design their economy without too much expense or outside intervention. The town council accepted the plan and Kinsale became the first Transition Town. Rob then moved to Totnes in Devon, and with one or two others started a Transition movement there, which has now spread around the world.

The attraction of the Transition movement is that it rests on practical and local initiatives to meet the challenge not only of peak oil,[2] but also of climate change and of the ongoing financial and economic crisis. Whether you are threatened by increasingly violent storms in North America, by rising sea levels in the Pacific (where many island communities are already dispossessed), by unemployment in southern Europe, or disturbed by rising levels of inequality in Europe or North America, a great many people sense that 'business as usual' is not an option but do not know how to go about doing things differently. Transition offers a way of thinking with others about these issues and taking action at a local level.

As Transition Edinburgh puts it, a Transition group 'connects and supports community groups, and initiates practical projects that strive for a greener, fairer, healthier and more resilient town, city or village'. More broadly, in the words of Transition Manchester, the aim of a Transition group is to

- drastically reduce carbon emissions (in response to climate change)
- significantly rebuild resilience (in response to peak oil)
- greatly strengthen our local economy (in response to economic instability).

The Transition Town Movement takes the challenges of peak oil, climate change, and the faltering of the present

---

2 The point in time when the maximum rate of petroleum extraction is reached, after which the rate of production is expected to slowly decline.

economic model not as a threat but a promise. Hopkins talks not only of energy descent (becoming less dependent on oil) but of energy ascent, as the community mobilizes, finds its creativity and learns to work together for the common good. The assumption is that the future can be shaped so that it is preferable to the present. Each step down the oil dependent hill, he argues, could be a step towards sanity, towards a greater recognition of the value of the place we find ourselves in (city, town or village) and towards wholeness.

The Transition movement is not primarily a campaigning movement but a *community building movement*. At an early meeting of the movement in Totnes a speaker was asked what the single most important thing was that someone could do to respond to these challenges, and the answer was, 'Join the choir!' It works on the premise that:

- If we wait for governments, it will be too little too late.
- If we act as individuals, it will be too little.
- If we act as communities, it might be just enough, just in time.

All over the world this premise is energizing and appealing because all over the world (not just in Britain) there is widespread disenchantment with mainstream politics and its power to deliver. The 'P' word (politics) is more or less absent from Transition literature and discussion, but in fact Transition is about citizens shaping their world (their 'polis'). Transition is not about retreat to some imagined rural past but envisages a future where the local, national or international are better balanced than at present. So, for example, at the international level it certainly wants strong worldwide climate change protocols, and a moratorium on biodiesel production. But at the same time it wants much more power devolved to local communities. Not aligned to any political party, Transition works to change the cultural story, to make unelectable policies electable, to lead by example and action rather than by hectoring. Rooted in permaculture, it seeks *practical, realizable steps* here and now which ordinary people can take to make society more resilient. It is not anti-technology, but pro appropriate technology. Recently it has enthusiastically embraced social entrepreneurship – the idea that all the energy, imagination and drive of the entrepreneur can be harnessed not to make profits for an individual or a company but for the good of the community.

Although it does not accept that economic growth is the answer to all our problems, it is not a hairshirt, tighten your belts, 'let's do without' movement, but believes that a more satisfying, creative and community oriented way of life can be found than we currently experience.

In terms of *process* it is profoundly democratic, aiming at consensus decision making, and using 'technologies' like open space and world café, in which there is the minimum of centralized control. It seeks to be inclusive, and to deal with the potential sense of powerlessness people feel in the face of large problems by celebrating both success and failure. It wants to create safe spaces for people to talk, think and act. The ethos is respectful but with an emphasis on enjoyment and creativity. Key to the ethos is the idea that Transition should provide a vision of a society so enticing that people will want to join in.

Since we can only get somewhere if we know where we are going, Transition asks people to imagine where they would like their place or community to be in five, ten, 20, 50 years' time. It tries to steer a course between the apocalyptic (social chaos, local warlordism) and the starry eyed (a hi tech, zero carbon future). This means it has an 'earth steward' perspective: given the renewable resources we have at our disposal and given the creative power of communities, what might the world look like? The focus is resilience – the ability to adapt and thrive in the face of changes. Transition groups explore the practical creation of possible resilient futures in many dimensions. Most Transition groups have sub-groups that focus particular people's energies and enthusiasms. As Transition Lancaster puts it, the interest groups are what makes Transition buzz.

So, for example, all Transition groups are concerned about *energy* and look for ways to set in place local energy schemes in their locality. Probably the most popular and most successful area is *food*, and many groups have started local allotment schemes or got involved with community-supported agriculture. Eating local food helps support the local economy in maintaining local jobs and shops. *Transport* is another major concern, and many Transition groups campaign for better cycle routes and better public transport, and encourage car sharing and the use of car clubs. Many Transition groups have interest groups reflecting on *the economy*. Of the many international and national changes needed to build a planet friendly, just and stable economic system, some part of the solution needs to be the creation of resilient and sustainable local economies. A resilient society, many analysts argue, is a fairer and more just society, a key part of why many people are involved in Transition. In many parts of Europe and North America, *housing* costs have rocketed over the past 40 years, making housing a tremendous burden for the low paid. The building industry is also one of the key emitters of greenhouse gases. To address this, many groups, including Transition groups, are starting Community Land Trusts, which provide low-cost housing owned by the community and not available for the speculative profit making which has characterized the housing market recently.

Resilience demands different practices but it is also what we call a spiritual matter, which is why many groups have people who focus on *inner Transition*. What are the spiritual resources of the Transition process? How do we keep going when the challenges seem so immense? How do we avoid despair? Inner Transition often draws on work such as Joanna Macy's, which through its techniques of individual and group creative learning can help inform the way in which we learn through meditation, prayer and discussion.

Many Christians are already involved in the Transition process. Jonathan Jelfs, Interfaith minister and member of Transition Liverpool, says:

> It seems to me that religion and spirituality have always been about Transition, expressed in such terms as being born again, conversion, repentance, awakening and enlightenment. In other words, Transition has a spiritual heart. It has also been clear that any such transition will always affect both the inner and outer aspects of reality – a change of mind and heart and also a change in behaviour and action.

Church policies already call their members to change the way they live, with guidelines on living more sustainably, ways to 'green' church buildings, still more on sharing resources. The longstanding tradition of recycling (which church fête does not include selling or exchanging 'jumble', the sharing of food and the recycling of books?) and acting locally (facilitating fêtes, concerts and shows) already demonstrate the culture of resilience that the Transition message adumbrates. At the Catholic Peace and Justice Conference in 2011 a delegate spoke of Transition as 'a great movement of the Spirit'. In this book we want to encourage Christians to get involved in Transition. We also want to encourage church communities to think of themselves as Transition communities, and as such to get involved with Transition initiatives in their area. It goes without saying that there should on no account be specifically Christian Transition groups, but our view is that the emphases of the Transition movement are close to many of the core Christian emphases over the centuries. We outline these in what follows as an invitation to Christian communities to get involved in Transition. Effectively what we are doing is setting out our view of a Christian account of inner Transition, drawing on the narratives and themes of Christian tradition, trying to highlight how consonant the emphases of Transition are with the Christian narrative, while at the same time acknowledging that churches and Christians can learn a great deal from engagement in this movement.

# 2

# The NAME

In thinking about why and how Church might engage with Transition we need to begin by thinking about the heart of Christian vision and values, the idea of 'God'. The word 'God' in any language is the generic term for the origin and end of all things. It seems probable that at an early stage of human history most humans had 'earth religions' of one kind or another which reverenced the sacredness of all life. This might have been animist (perceiving spirit in trees, or animals – whatever is immediately around) or it might have been pantheist (believing that divine Spirit was present in all things), but it was probably local. Then, according to the philosopher Karl Jaspers, sometime around the sixth century BCE, and following the growth of cities and of trade, there was an 'axial moment' around the world in which these were left behind for various ways of construing the one reality behind the diversity of phenomena, conceived differently in China by Confucius, in India by Gautama and earlier by Aryan sages, in Greece by philosophers beginning with Heraclitus, and in Israel by the prophets.

According to the story telling of Israel, 'God' disclosed Godself to someone called Moshe (Moses) when the group from which he came found itself in a situation of slave labour in Egypt. We don't know how old the story is, and as it is, it is highly edited, but it is certainly theologically very sophisticated. 'Moshe' is an Egyptian name. (Freud wrote a famous essay in which he claimed that Moshe was an Egyptian and he read many of the peculiarities of Jewish faith out of that.) The biblical narrative tells us that Moshe was a Hebrew boy brought up in the household of Pharaoh. It gives us to understand therefore that Moshe was inculturated as an Egyptian but that he knew himself to be ethnically a Hebrew. Seeing at first hand the oppression of his kin he intervenes and kills an Egyptian who is beating a Hebrew, but finds that it earns him no thanks. He is, after all, a rich outsider – what is it to do with him? Finding his crime discovered he flees into the 'wilderness' – socio-symbolic space for the area outside of the ruling assumptions of Egypt.

This is the first really interesting point of the story. When John the Baptist and Jesus went into the 'wilderness' they were seeking a standpoint outside of the ruling assumptions of the Roman empire and of the Jewish opposition groups. In the same way we today need a space outside of the ruling assumptions of neo-liberalism – that there has to be growth, that austerity is the way to deal with economic collapse, that there is a technological answer to everything. In this sense the Transition movement provides a revelatory space – a space to think otherwise and to think together.

Moshe works for some years in this alternative culture and at the end of that time he has this famous encounter:

Moshe was keeping the flock of his father-in-law Jethro, the priest of Midian; he led his flock beyond the wilderness, and came to Horeb, the mountain of God. There the angel of the LORD appeared to him in a flame of fire out of a bush; he looked, and the bush was blazing, yet it was not consumed. Then Moshe said, 'I must turn aside and look at this great sight, and see why the bush is not burned up.' When the LORD saw that he had turned aside to see, God called to him out of the bush, 'Moses, Moses!' And he said, 'Here I am.' ... Then the LORD said, 'I have observed the misery of my people who are in Egypt; I have heard their cry on account of their taskmasters. Indeed, I know their sufferings, and I have come down to deliver them from the Egyptians ... But Moshe said to God, 'Who am I that I should go to Pharaoh, and bring the Israelites out of Egypt?' He said, 'I will be with you' ... But Moshe said to God, 'If I come to the Israelites and say to them, "The God of your ancestors has sent me to you", and they ask me, "What is his name?" what shall I say to them?' God said to Moshe, 'I AM WHO I AM.' ... This is my name for ever, and this my title for all generations.

What God says to Moshe is '*Ehyeh ashe ehyeh*', usually translated these days as 'I am who I will be', and meaning that who God is will be disclosed in the process of liberation, in the course of the journey. The Hebrew letters for this disclosure, YHWH, are the basis of the old translation 'Jehovah'. From the beginning Jews would never use the NAME, but referred to it by circumlocutions, in particular Adonai, Lord. In the Synagogue Jews refer to God as 'the NAME', and we will follow that practice here. The fact that the Name of God is unspeakable and the voice of God cannot be tied down is about resistance to colonization by any idol. It is also a way of saying that the origin and end of all things can only be known through a narrative – not just any old narrative, but a particular narrative of the movement from slavery to freedom.

Transition is a passage from one state to another: in terms of the exodus narrative, from slavery to freedom. To be Christian is to be called fundamentally to such a transition, understood through the ages rather individualistically as a journey or a pilgrimage (as, for example, in John Bunyan's *The Pilgrim's Progress*). The Transition movement offers us a particular construal of another transition, another journey or movement between states needed for all human beings, but especially for citizens in the rich North if they are going to adapt peacefully and constructively to the new conditions when cheap and readily available oil can no longer be taken for granted. Inner Transition is about the spiritual resources for the journey. For Christians this will include an understanding of the journeying God, the God of the Exodus, who calls people out of their slavery to consumerism.

This takes us on to another part of the narrative of the Exodus. The book we call Numbers arises from a situation of civil war. It reflects on multiple challenges to leadership, and despair of ever arriving at a situation of peace and justice. On their journey people were fed with manna. This is often referred to as something delicious, just what we are always wanting; but that is not how the exodus generation saw it, at least according to this story:

The rabble among them had a strong craving; and the Israelites also wept again, and said, 'If only we had meat to eat! We remember the fish we used to eat in Egypt for nothing, the cucumbers, the melons, the leeks, the onions, and the garlic; but now our strength is dried up, and there is nothing at all but this manna to look at.'

The rabble (which is all of us) craves what the supermarkets can give us. We don't want to pay the price of freedom. Many inner Transition groups wrestle with the problem of what to do about consumerism. They think of it in terms of addiction, and often use the twelve-step model to think about how to break free from that. As the African American proverb puts it, 'It is easier to get the people out of Egypt than to get Egypt out of the people.' The story makes the assumption that freedom is costly, and that there is a choice between well-fed slavery on the one hand, and the long road to freedom on the other. The story tells us that the NAME calls us to that long road, to a transitus. At the far end is 'the land of milk and honey', which is to say, a world of redeemed relationships, a world where people respect and honour one another as equals. This is what Christians pray for when they pray 'Your Kingdom come'. That prayer takes us straight into Transition – progress to a state of shalom, of peace and justice, in which the needs of all people and of God's good earth are honoured.

There is another part of the exodus story which bears on Transition. According to the story, Moshe goes up Mount Horeb and stays there so long that people think he may have disappeared or died:

When the people saw that Moshe delayed to come down from the mountain, the people gathered around Aaron, and said to him, 'Come, make gods for us, who shall go before us; as for this Moshe, the man who brought us up out of the land of Egypt, we do not know what has become of him.' Aaron said to them, 'Take off the gold rings that are on the ears of your wives, your sons, and your daughters, and bring them to me.' So all the people took off the gold rings from their ears, and brought them to Aaron. He took the gold from them, formed it in a mould, and cast an image of a calf; and they said, 'These are your gods, O Israel, who brought you up out of the land of Egypt!' When Aaron saw this, he built an altar before it; and Aaron made proclamation and said, 'Tomorrow shall be a festival to the LORD.' They rose early the next day, and offered burnt offerings and brought sacrifices of well-being; and the people sat down to eat and drink, and rose up to revel.

In the economy of the writers of this story gold is a means of exchange, a means of preserving value and a measure of value: it is the centre of gravity of the economy. Aaron makes an image out of it; he reifies the economy and makes it a cultic object, he fetishes gold. The embodiment of economics (gold) is set up as God of the whole world – that is the process recounted here. Throughout Scripture there is a contest between the NAME, the God of life, and 'idols'. Idols are not harmless 'green eyed yellow' statues to the north of Kathmandu, or anywhere else; they are real forces which call for our absolute loyalty and commitment. This had already been seen by Martin Luther, who, commenting on the first commandment, said that the faith of the heart makes both God and idol. He went on:

> A God is that to which we look for all good and in which we find refuge in every time of need ... Many a person thinks he has God and everything he needs when he has money and property; in them he trusts and of them he boasts so stubbornly and securely that he cares for no one. Surely such a man also has a god – mammon by name, that is, money and possessions – on which he fixes his whole heart. It is the most common idol on earth.[1]

'Competitiveness for unlimited money accumulation', says Heidelberg professor of theology Ulrich Duchrow, 'is the objective and subjective structure, the "god" of our market society, which determines the whole'. It is this god that is driving the rise in global temperature which could lead to the end of human life on earth; which lies behind the sweat shops, and which can crucify whole nations through debt. 'Accordingly,' says Duchrow, 'the core of what we must reject is the absolute value attributed to competition and the total absence of limits set on the cancerous growth of capital.'[2] Absolute value and absence of limits are traditional attributes of deity. Idolatry is about making absolute that which is not God. The golden calf is a 'really existing god', with real power, which has to be celebrated in liturgies that internalize its lordship, and to defy it means you have to be cast into the fire, as the opponents of Pinochet

---

1 Exposition of the First Commandment in the Large Catechism.
2 Ulrich Duchrow, *Alternatives to Global Capitalism: Drawn from Biblical History, Designed for Political Action*, Utrecht: International Books, 1995, p. 234.

and the other Latin American dictators were cast into the fire. Every generation is confronted with its own idols, who grab power over them and seek to devour them. Our own idol is the doctrine of necessary economic growth. Of course all of us in the 'developed' world are beneficiaries of the growth that has taken place since 1750. Of course growth is necessary to raise the living standards of billions of the world's people. But if growth is at the expense of generations yet unborn then it is idolatrous, and this is the charge.

In Scripture the NAME is always spoken of as 'the living God' because God is the source of all life and wills life. In Deuteronomy, another book that takes the journey from slavery to freedom as its framework, Israel is offered 'two ways', a way of death and a way of life, and the story ends, 'Choose life!' Transition does not work with this stark choice, but the urgency of the movement comes from the fact that peak oil and climate change could in fact mean death for millions if they are simply ignored. Many witnesses from Pacific island communities already speak of the threat to their lives of climate change. Effectively, in its work on energy, food, transport, housing, and especially on alternative economics, Transition is also urging people to 'choose life'.

## Questions for discussion

- How should the word 'God' be understood?

- If 'the faith and trust of the heart make both god and idol', as Luther puts it, what are the gods and idols of our society?

- What might be a contemporary analogy to the biblical story of the Exodus?

# 3

# The Way

In English we are used to the question, 'Do you go to church?' In most settlements you can ask the question, 'Where is the church?', meaning a building. These questions would be impossible in the New Testament. The Greek word for church is *ekklesia*, and that in turn translates the Hebrew word *quahal*. Both of these words are primarily political. The *ekklesia* was the assembly of free citizens in Athens, when they met to debate and discuss policy. The *quahal YHWH* was the assembly of the tribes of Israel, where they too met to determine what they should do. One of the best established facts about Jesus was that he chose twelve disciples, the purpose of which was to symbolically re-constitute Israel. It was an act of prophetic symbolism. Why? What for? What did he hope for?

Jesus begins his ministry by calling disciples, a word that means learner or apprentice. What they learn are the values and practices of 'the kingdom of God'. The metaphor of the kingdom is difficult to understand for people who do not live under monarchs or accept the hierarchical order kingdoms imply. The biblical scholar and social activist Ched Myers borrows a phrase from Kentucky farmer, novelist, poet and essayist Wendell Berry and talks about 'the Great

Economy', meaning a world ordered according to the nature and values of the NAME. We learn in Matthew that disciples are not to be angry, not to resist evil doers, not to make a song and dance about almsgiving or piety, not to worry about how they are to live or to be clothed, or what they will eat, not to amass property, to order their sexual desires, to learn to forgive those who offend them or even hate them, and not to judge. In such teaching Jesus seeks to constitute a discipleship community that will model an alternative way of living and ordering society – which is why he uses the metaphors of salt and light to speak of the community. All this he understood as simply filling out the implications of Torah. Then he sent them out – to be an apostle is simply to be sent (from the Greek verb *apostelein*, to send) – to witness to the new reality he sensed the NAME was bringing into being, the 'reign of God'. When the disciples asked how to pray Jesus responded, 'pray for the coming of God's kingdom on earth, as in heaven'. In Chapter 1 we mentioned Transition's commitment to 'visioning' the future. This applies to prayer. The future, writes the North American theologian Walter Wink, 'belongs to whoever can envision in the manifold of its potentials a new and desirable possibility, which faith then fixes upon as inevitable'. History belongs to the intercessors, who believe the future into being.[1]

The disciples, the ones who have been taught all this, follow Jesus on the way that leads to the realization of the kingdom (or Great Economy), and Luke tells us that

---

1 Walter Wink, *Engaging the Powers*, Minneapolis: Fortress, 1992, p. 299.

the earliest name for Christianity was 'the Way'. So the discipleship community, the *ekklesia,* is literally a movement whose task it is to witness to what the NAME is up to by way of creating a new world and to invite people to join this movement. The movement begins with repentance, which means discontinuity with the established order. The established order is class divided and admires power and privilege. The discipleship community is expected to live by service and to live in solidarity with the poor. The established order lives by division, whether of pure and impure, rich and poor, native and immigrant. The discipleship community refuses to accept that: 'those who are not against us are for us', says Jesus in Mark's Gospel. The Great Economy is not built by sectarian division but by embracing those on the margins.

The ethos of the discipleship community is one of service. One of the earliest leaders of the community, Paul, writes, 'Have this mind in you which was in Christ Jesus who, because he had the form of God [not 'despite having the form of God', as is usually translated] did not hang on to it but took the form of a slave'. For the whole of the early church riches barred a person from discipleship. Jesus said that it was impossible for a rich person to be a disciple for the simple reason that in the Great Economy there are no rich and poor, just as Deuteronomy and Leviticus envisaged.

Jesus also described his disciples as his friends. 'Friends' in the ancient world were not people who signed up on your Facebook page, or people you met in the pub, but the very basis of political community. We get a sense of this in the

Quaker use of the word 'Friend'. It is not an emotional tie but signifies belonging to the same movement, sharing the same values.

Paul took from Jesus his understanding of a radical new beginning in human affairs but he expressed it differently. He talked about a new creation, and thought that in Jesus human history had made a fresh start with a new Adam. Practically speaking, Paul envisaged *ekklesia* as a new movement that would break down the fundamental divisions of humanity. As a Jew he was used to dismissing non-Jews as Gentiles. In *ekklesia*, he came to see there could be no Jew or Gentile. The fact that messiah Jesus took the form of a slave meant that the class division which was so profound in his world (slaves had no rights, and Aristotle had doubted they were truly human) meant that class was also abolished. As a man Paul doubtless grew up with patriarchal prejudices, and some people suspect that he retained them, but certainly on a good day he believed that in *ekklesia* male and female no longer counted.

To describe the reality of this movement Paul took over a metaphor familiar from the ancient history of Rome, harking back to the story of how Menenius Agrippa quelled a riot by the plebs by reminding them that they were all part of one body. But Agrippa made a fundamental distinction between different parts of the body – superior and inferior parts. The Senate, he told the mob, was the superior part, and they could not manage without it. Paul does something quite different:

As it is, there are many members, yet one body. The eye cannot say to the hand, 'I have no need of you', nor again the head to the feet, 'I have no need of you'. On the contrary, the members of the body that seem to be weaker are indispensable, and those members of the body that we think less honourable we clothe with greater honour, and our less respectable members are treated with greater respect; whereas our more respectable members do not need this. But God has so arranged the body, giving the greater honour to the inferior member, that there may be no dissension within the body, but the members may have the same care for one another. If one member suffers, all suffer together with it; if one member is honoured, all rejoice together with it.

So this is a body in which the lowliest are most esteemed – just as Jesus had envisaged. Paul's account of the body was egalitarian in a way that the Roman story was not and historically this is something that the discipleship community (right up to today) has not managed to comprehend or accept.

In a later letter, which may not be by Paul, the metaphor is changed so that Christ is understood as the head of the body, a metaphor that was used 'to attack at its deepest cosmic and psychological roots the perennial human habit of accepting as ultimate the world's way of dividing humankind into competing societies, whether religious, racial, cultural or economic'.[2]

---

2 Paul Minear, *Images of the Church in the New Testament*, Louisville: Westminster John Knox Press, 1960.

The body was characterized by *koinonia*, fellowship, which meant shared wealth as well as worship. A famous description from the second century tells how Christian groups were known for their mutual support, so that people said, 'See how those Christians love one another.' We could be tempted to regard that as self-congratulatory were it not that a hostile witness, second-century pagan philosopher Celsus, grudgingly confirms it.

There are analogies between the vision and task of the discipleship community and those of the Transition movement. Transition also seeks to build connections, break down inequalities and give a voice to everyone. Like Paul it assumes that everyone has something to offer and everyone has something to learn. It recognizes that it can learn from low-income communities and work with them to overcome poverty and exclusion. Food, energy bills and health are just some of the concerns. Workshops run by Transition groups show people how to insulate their homes cheaply so that they can reduce their energy bills. In Totnes, 70 per cent of houses in the town's solar panel scheme belonged to low-income families. Tooting and Finsbury Park in London have put diversity at the heart of whatever they do, and interfaith initiatives have done much to encourage the emergence of, for example, community gardens and cross-community engagement.

Social inclusion and justice are fundamental themes of Christian witness, and Christian members of Transition groups need to bring this passion for justice with them. Social and environmental inclusion are ways to help us to be reconciled with each other, the earth and God.

To use the language of the New Testament, we can say that human ecological systems will only work if each of us works together to ensure reconciliation. The Anglican Church adopts as one of the 'five marks of mission' the quest to 'transform unjust structures of society, to challenge violence of every kind and to pursue peace and reconciliation'.[3] To the extent it is seeking shalom – wholesome communities in a wholesome relation with the planet – Transition shares this vision.

The focus on community in the New Testament was later re-emphasized as the doctrine of God developed. For Jewish Christians like Paul of Tarsus the resurrection meant that Jesus was in some extraordinary way identical with the NAME. He has received, says Paul, 'the Name above every Name'. In the light of that event the Jews and Gentiles who joined the new movement prayed in a different way: they prayed 'to the Father, through the Son, in the Spirit'. The attempt to explain that practice led to the development of the doctrine of the Trinity. For Christians 'Trinity' is the Name of God, as recognized in the beautiful eighth-century Irish poem, 'St Patrick's breastplate':

> I bind unto myself today
> The strong Name of the Trinity,
> By invocation of the same
> The Three in One and One in Three.

Like the passage in Exodus, the poem makes clear that to speak about God is to tell a story. The story of the exodus is not eliminated – it remains, but it is glossed by a further

---

3 Bonds of Affection, Anglican Consultative Council, 1984.

story, the story of the life, death and resurrection of Jesus, and the story of whatever it is we mean by 'Spirit'. This story, summed up by the NAME, is what Christians mean by the word 'God'. The story is not simply past, but continuing. It invites us into it. Indeed, we are part of it.

Reflecting on the Trinitarian NAME, Christians have understood it in a particular way. The NAME points to the fact that the origin and end of all things is relationship in itself. This is by no means a self-evident truth. Some religions insist on the absolute oneness and aloneness of God. Some envisage the end of all things in terms of un-differentiated unity. The NAME says that relationships and community are ontologically ultimate – that all things whatsoever, from the Higgs boson (supposing it exists), to the lowliest microbe, to human beings, to angels (supposing they exist), come out of and return to relationship. Of course the relationships of sub-atomic particles and those of human beings are different. Nevertheless it is clear that we live in a relational universe in which nothing works outside of relationship. Like the biologist Theodore Dobzhansky, we can think of a hierarchy of levels that open upwards but cannot be reduced downwards (the mistake of much reductionist thinking among some natural scientists): relationships at the level of sub-atomic particles are transcended and embraced at the chemical level; these in turn at the biological level; these in turn at the social level of human relations; and all are embraced in the relational reality of the NAME.

According to the Christian understanding, relationship is ultimate, and not just any relationship, or relationship as a principle, but a relationship of love, in which love fulfils love, so that as we read in John's Gospel the Father is the Father because the Son is the Son, and the Spirit is the Spirit because the Father and the Son are who they are, and so on for all three persons.

All this bears on Transition because one of the great themes of the movement is the building of more resilient communities. Christianity has lived with the call to community for 2,000 years, and experienced the difficulty of forming it from the start. In the New Testament we read of sharp divisions and quarrels in the discipleship community from the very beginning. As Christianity became the religion of empire it made more and more preposterous claims to power, in clean contradiction to the gospels it read day by day. Formed as a community of forgiveness which knew no limit ('until seventy times seven'), different groups anathematized one another, burned those with whom they disagreed from the eleventh century on and, in the seventeenth century, could wipe out the population of an entire city, men, women and children, if they belonged to the wrong denomination (at Magdeburg). Formed as a community in opposition to Mammon, it acquired stupendous wealth and even formed its own banks! No wonder that Voltaire, in the next century, said, 'écrasez l'Infame!' Although Christians no longer burn one another there are still deeply inhuman and unloving acts performed in the name of the 'church' day by day (see, for example, Norman Lewis' account of *The Missionaries*).[4]

---

4 Norman Lewis, *The Missionaries: God Against the Indians*, London: Penguin, 1990.

What remains, then, of the original vision? We might think of it as a plant or tree that has been cut right down, poisoned, where every attempt has been made to kill it, but where beautiful new shoots still spring up. Human examples are the Taizé community in France, the Jubilee debt campaign, the work of the Sisters of Charity in Calcutta, the many martyrs in Latin America resisting the tyranny of neo-liberalism, the work of the World Council of Churches in calling for urgent action to address climate change now for more than 40 years. Despite the dreadful history the call to understand the NAME at work seeking a new kind of human reality still has its power.

There are many differences between the discipleship community and Transition – above all, as we shall see shortly, is the question of worship, but it should be clear that both movements share a vision of a different, a more just and a more whole human future. Church communities can learn much from the Transition approach to inner resilience and wellbeing. But churches have much to bring to Transition, especially in their passion for justice and in their understanding of the praxis of forgiveness. A discipleship community (church or congregation) which embraces Transition could be a beacon of resilience, as well as of social and environmental justice, in its community. If each discipleship community sent one or two members to take part in Transition training, the skills and methods of Transition could enhance the activity of the church community – not just in practical organizational matters but also in spiritual wellbeing.

In translating *'ekklesia'* as 'discipleship community' we are not suggesting that institutionalization was wholly mistaken. Institutions are necessary to survive over time. However, the Reformation rightly insisted that the church is *semper reformanda* – always in the process of reformation. Re-discovering itself as a discipleship community is part of that reformation today, and in this process learning from Transition, and being part of that initiative, can play a valuable part and recall the community to some of its founding insights, values and commitments.

## Questions for discussion

- How could your congregation contribute to the building of a more resilient community?
- What would it mean, concretely, to witness to reconciliation in present day society?

# 4

# Serving Creation

In the book of Daniel, chapter 3, after the story of Shadrach, Meshach and Abednego, there is an ancient interpolation, usually omitted in modern versions, known to scholars as the 'Song of the Three Children', but to generations of worshippers at mattins as the 'Benedicite'. The Benedicite is a huge, rambling, baroque shout of joy at the beauty and wonder of creation in which snow, ice, hail, frost, fire, earth, stars, sun and moon, showers and dews, winds, fire and heat all praise the Lord:

O ye Winter and Summer, bless ye the Lord: praise and exalt him above all for ever.
O ye mountains and little hills, bless ye the Lord: praise and exalt him above all for ever.
O all ye things that grow on the earth, bless ye the Lord: praise and exalt him above all for ever.
O ye fountains, bless ye the Lord: praise and exalt him above all for ever.
O ye seas and rivers, bless ye the Lord: praise and exalt him above all for ever.
O ye whales and all that move in the waters, bless ye the Lord: praise and exalt him above all for ever.

O all ye fowls of the air, bless ye the Lord: praise and
exalt him above all for ever.
O all ye beasts and cattle, bless ye the Lord: praise and
exalt him above all for ever.

Only when the whole of non-human creation has praised
God are humans invited to join in, both together as one
choir of praise. It is God centred, not human centred. The
whole of creation praises God, and humans are seen as
part of the community of creation. Inner Transition has a
good deal to say about 'nature', about learning from it and
respecting it. The idea of nature is very complex, and in
its contemporary usage owes a great deal to romanticism.
For Christians, all reality, both human and non-human, is
'grace', gift, the product of the love and creativity of the
NAME. This is the basis of their understanding of, and
approach to, the non-human world.

In 1967 medieval historian Lynn White wrote a notori-
ous article in which he claimed that the 'dominion text'
– Genesis 1.26: 'have dominion over the earth and sub-
due it' – lay at the root of the ecological crisis because it
licensed Europeans to regard the earth as their possession.
This claim was often run together with Francis Bacon's
talk of 'putting nature to the test'. The influence of the
article has been in inverse proportion to its plausibility.
In fact Christianity from the start was in fierce opposition
to cultural movements that felt that matter was disgusting
and manual work degrading. It affirmed the goodness of
creation and understood it as gift. In the ancient world toil
was only for the low born. The high born were warriors,
philosophers and landowners. Benedict of Nursia, one of

the great figures in European history, taught a new respect for creation through the dignity of labour. When someone came to join the order they were given a spade or a hoe and sent into the garden. Many stumbled at this and turned away. The Benedictine order and its offshoots were early permaculturists and their work laid the foundation for the recovery of European populations after the dark ages. As someone who practised the *lectio divina* (the daily reading of Scripture), Benedict knew that the 'dominion text' was qualified by the passage that follows – Genesis 2.15, which understands human beings as gardeners and tells them to serve and to 'keep' creation in the same way that they had to 'keep' the commandments. The ethos of service which characterized community relations also applied to relations with the non-human world – which may explain why, right up to the present, Benedictine monks make such good beekeepers! It is later, with Descartes, that humans are described as 'masters and possessors' of nature, a view bound up with the rise of empirical science, and new views of the State and of the economy. There were many wonderful features of this development, to which we owe, for example, modern medicine, but the downside was the loss of the idea of creation as gift. This was signified for earlier Christians in the practice of 'grace' (saying thank you) at meals. That remained for some centuries, of course, but it was no longer recognized in eighteenth-century farming practice, in the enclosures, and in the way farm labour was treated. That was as alienated as anything in the factories.

The understanding of creation as gift can only be expressed as ontological – part of the very being of reality. Paul already spoke of the whole creation 'groaning in travail', in bondage to *phthora* – corruption, the second law of thermo-dynamics. He understood the resurrection as a promise not just to humans but to all reality. This insight was developed later in theologies of immanence, which understood the relationship of the divine Trinity sustaining all things in being. The German theologian Jürgen Moltmann, who was advocating an ecological theology even before *Limits to Growth* in 1972, writes:

> It is not elementary particles that are basic, as the mechanistic world view maintains, but the overriding harmony of the relations and of the self-transcending movements, in which the longing of the Spirit for a still unattained consummation finds expression. If the cosmic Spirit is the Spirit of God, the universe cannot be viewed as a closed system. It has to be understood as a system that is open – open for God and for God's future.[1]

The Benedicite follows the pattern of Genesis 1, ending with the Sabbath, which the Jewish writer Franz Rosenzweig described as 'the feast of creation'. Understood like this the Sabbath complements the image of the exodus. As we have seen, that understands human life as a journey or quest. The Sabbath, by contrast, understands the goal of all creation as celebration, a feast, leisure. From the start the Sabbath is understood as giving a break from labour not only for human beings – all of them, including slaves and migrant workers – but for the animals as well:

---

1 Jürgen Moltmann, *God in Creation*, London: SCM Press, 1984, p. 103.

Six days you shall labour and do all your work. But the seventh day is a sabbath to the NAME; you shall not do any work – you, your son or your daughter, your male or female slave, your livestock, or the alien resident in your towns.

The political freedom of exodus is complemented by the freedom of rest and celebration. Already in the first century the Roman historian Tacitus castigates the Jews for keeping this weekly strike. It is true that the Puritan 'sabbath' could often be a burden, but equally the rule that no work should be done once a week was a sign that life was not made for labour, a spoke in the wheel of the ceaseless productive process of capitalism, in which the wheels must never stop turning.

From the understanding of creation as gift and community, which at the same time sets people free from the remorseless round of toil, follows an eco-politics that challenges consumerism and calls people to change their lifestyle to one that prioritizes co-existence and co-operation rather than competition. For the Christian it is precisely understanding the world (what is often called 'nature') as God's creation, which is to say as gift, which means that an alternative way of living and dealing with other living things – we might say a Transition – has to be found. Another of the 'five marks of mission' we have mentioned is 'to strive to safeguard the integrity of creation and renew the life of the earth'. People from all sorts of traditions, secular and religious, recognize the ecological crisis as a spiritual crisis, a crisis of values. If the discipleship community could understand once again the proper import of its songs of praise, of the

Benedicite, it could throw its weight behind a new way of relating to the non-human world, one of the key requirements in addressing the ecological crisis, and one of the key concerns of transition.

## Questions for discussion

- How might an understanding of world as creation take shape in concrete practices in our community?

- What might the implications of this account of creation be for understanding practices of farming, building and finance?

# 5

# The Human One

At the heart of Christianity, of course, is the slightly shadowy figure of Jesus of Nazareth. 'Shadowy' because the gospels are not biographies and we can say little about Jesus' personality. We don't 'know' Jesus in the way we might say we 'know' our friends or contemporaries, or even someone like Augustine, about whom large biographies are written. But if Christians are going to talk about inner Transition they have to talk about Jesus – he is at the heart of what Christians believe the NAME has revealed to human beings.

There are certain things we can say for certain about Jesus. We know that he was crucified. The evidence is very strong that he was regarded as a teacher and healer. We know that at the heart of his teaching was the idea of the rule of God, or Great Economy. The gospels tell us he was a person who kept dubious company – collaborators and people a little too fond of the pleasures of the table. They also say that people recognized a special source of authority in him that didn't come from his education. Some people took him for a prophet. When he asked his disciples who they thought he was, one of them replied that he was *mashiach*, the anointed one, the one who would finally redeem all Israel's lost hopes, free them from the Romans, make them independent again, and so forth. Their view of him was probably pretty conventional: we overhear a conversation where one of them wants the job of Chancellor of the Exchequer and another one wants to be Home Secretary when the new regime is inaugurated. Jesus seems to have accepted the term '*mashiach*' (translated as the Greek 'Christos', now treated as a proper name, a sort of surname – when it is not used as a swear word), but he clearly radically re-interpreted it. The story of what happened in Gethsemane, and the word from the cross, 'My God, why have you forsaken me?', seems to suggest that he went on wrestling with the question of what on earth it might mean right until the end. The term Jesus himself uses most often is 'Son of Man', which Ched Myers translates as 'the Human One'. The term probably comes from Daniel, where it represents proper human government as opposed to the brutality of the reign of Antiochus Epiphanes, symbolized by the vision of monstrous beasts. In a world full of governments that routinely torture opponents, in which 'terrorists' are eliminated at will by drone and missile attacks, or by special forces, we can readily understand the appeal to a truly human way of doing things, symbolized by this figure, 'the Human One'.

All of this is relatively ordinary: there were many healers in the first century, many Rabbis, many prophets, many Messianic pretenders, and tens of thousands of people crucified. What sets Jesus apart and what originates the extraordinary – and to many nonsensical – journey of Christology, is the resurrection. Sometimes it is suggested that resurrection might have made sense in the first century, when people were so much more 'primitive', whereas it makes no sense now. This is contradicted in the New Testament itself. Luke tells us (we have no idea how historically accurate this is) that when Paul took his place in Speakers' Corner in Athens he got quite a hearing – people could understand the ethics – until he got to the resurrection, when they left to go to the pub or the café, or to return to work, on the assumption that he was self-evidently round the bend. Things are no different today. And it is true that if one chooses to believe in the resurrection the threads for doing so are slender. Christians believe because the earliest community obviously believed and cast around for ways to make sense of this preposterous claim. Some theologians have argued that we learn from Paul's conversion that the resurrection appearances were clearly visions. Paul insists that he too had a resurrection experience and so all the stories are in fact accounts of visions. The resurrection stories are therefore accounts of religious experiences. But visions were two-a-penny in the first century, and perfectly respectable. Why make life difficult for yourself with a preposterous claim if you don't have to? That is not meant as a 'proof' that the resurrection happened – there is no such thing. It's simply an awkward question arising from the New Testament. Accepting the resurrection is part of the practice of following the more difficult reading. It is here that the decision lies. Once accepted it is not difficult to make sense of theologically (on the grounds that the universe is sustained by the NAME, is proper to it, and that therefore the resurrection is no arbitrary intervention but an indication of what is always the case). The question is whether one chooses to accept it or not and this is primarily about being part of a community and a tradition. 'I handed down to you as of first importance what I in turn received,' says Paul, and he goes on to argue that without the resurrection there is no Christian community. It is the life of the community that constitutes the plausibility structure of the claim. No one has put this better than Myers in his great study of discipleship.[1] The resurrection stories begin, he says, with hope crushed, an experience we all know. We all have our own experiences of betrayal and tragedy, of apathy and overwhelming odds, of oppression and senseless suffering, which forces us to recognize that the world cannot really be changed after all. A stone is put against the grave, denying even the possibility of the usual rituals of mourning. But then the disciples find the stone rolled away. 'This aperture of hope against hope suggests that there might be a future for this story after all.' A figure dressed in white addresses them:

> Don't be incredulous. You're looking for Jesus of Nazareth, I presume. Yes, they killed him; they put him in here. But he's gone on. See for yourself. He's gone on ahead of you.

In Jesus' empty tomb, comments Myers, 'there is nothing but the ghost of our discipleship past and our discipleship future ... Whoever would follow Jesus must still take up the cross because this is the only practice powerful enough to deconstruct and reconstruct the world ... Easter celebrates the restoration of the narrative of biblical radicalism, which like Jesus goes on before us.' The disciples are

---

1 Ched Myers, *Who Will Roll Away the Stone?*, Maryknoll: Orbis, 1994.

sent back to Galilee. 'The geography of Easter is not in-
determinate or otherworldly (that is, dis-placed). No, it is
back in Galilee, where we were first called from denial to
discontinuity. The third call to discipleship invites us to re-
placement among our own story, land and people.'[2]

As noted in the discussion of the NAME, the resurrection
taught Christians a quite different way of thinking about
God. This was worked out in the doctrine of the Trinity,
but even more in Christology. Here Christians were led to
the equally ludicrous and problematic assertion that a given
human being, Jesus of Nazareth, was at the same time the
presence of the origin and end of all things in human space
and time. How on earth could that be? That was the question the doctrine of the incarnation was formulated to give
an answer to. In fact the doctrine of the incarnation is primarily a way of thinking about God. One can begin from
the concept of a supreme being who has all the attributes
necessary to be the creator of the universe – omnipotent,
omniscient and so forth. If we begin there we will never
understand the incarnation, however. Suppose we begin
from Jesus of Nazareth. Then a different understanding of
the NAME emerges. What does it mean to be God? What
is the divine 'nature'? The answer by the Swiss theologian
Karl Barth is: 'the free love, the omnipotent mercy, the
holy patience of the Father, Son and Holy Spirit'.[3] This
divine essence or nature totally determines who Jesus of
Nazareth is. Who he is, is totally determined by the grace
of God. This means on the one hand that it is possible to

2 Myers, *Who Will Roll Away the Stone?*, p. 410ff.
3 Karl Barth, *Church Dogmatics IV/2*, Edinburgh: T & T Clark,
1958, p. 234.

look at Jesus and say that he is God for us, but also to say that he is fully human because it is genuinely human to live by the grace of God.

What follows from this, as the early church fathers saw very clearly, is a passionate affirmation of bodies, of the earth, of material. 'Do not disparage matter,' said John, Chancellor of the Exchequer to the Caliph of Baghdad, 'for in Christ God took matter upon himself for our sake.' In his novel *The Unbearable Lightness of Being*, Milan Kundera explores this whole debate. In the second century a certain Valentinus was unable to accept Christ's full humanity on the grounds that it would be impossible to think that God could become human and could defecate. 'Shit' is the opposite of the divine. The church, however, insisted that no form of matter was unclean. Religious kitsch, Kundera points out, is the church going back on that early insistence, finding it too uncomfortable to live with. Here we see the significance of the incarnation for our engagement with Transition. Why be involved with Transition? Because we care about creation, and about our neighbour, and those who come after. Ours is often called a material culture. Wrong, says Wendell Berry. The way we treat matter shows that we do not value it enough. To believe in the incarnation is to treasure matter as that which the NAME not only created but took upon itself. In one of the most famous of the parables Jesus tells his disciples that the way they treat the poor, the hungry, the imprisoned, is the way they treat him. But in virtue of the incarnation this applies to the whole of creation: recycling, not flying, joining a movement that seeks to steward the earth and not abuse it is a response to the one who took matter for our sake.

## Questions for discussion

- What might follow from belief in the incarnation for the way we shape our local communities?

- What might follow from belief in the resurrection for our understanding of history, and of how change happens?

# 6

# A Domination Free Order

The single most comprehensive word to express salvation in the Hebrew Bible is 'shalom' (usually translated 'peace'). Salvation and shalom are virtually identical. Shalom may mean health, prosperity, peace from enemies. This theme is taken up in the gospels where salvation includes healing, restoring people to wholeness and, for Paul, living as part of a new type of community where tasks are shared, and the duty of mutual care is paramount. From a biblical perspective, what Transition seeks is shalom. How is this to be achieved? Most inner Transition groups focus on psychotherapy as a resource for healing, but the problem with this is that, like some accounts of Christian conversion, it wants to convert the world one by one. Most Christian narratives, on the other hand, talk about the cross of Christ. How might that relate to the establishment of shalom?

The letter to the Colossians, which may or may not be by Paul, has this to say about it:

> When you were dead in trespasses and the uncircumcision of your flesh, God made you alive together with him, when he forgave us all our trespasses, erasing the

record that stood against us with its legal demands. He set this aside, nailing it to the cross. He disarmed the rulers and authorities and made a public example of them, triumphing over them in it.

What is meant by 'rulers and authorities', or, as they are more familiarly known, 'principalities and powers'? In explaining these terms the North American theologian Walter Wink begins by outlining what he calls the 'domination system', founded on the idea of redemptive violence. This idea is very ancient – as found in Babylonian mythology – but it is equally contemporary, as in all Super Hero comics, Westerns, and many other forms of popular media.

> The psychodynamics of the television cartoon or comic book are marvellously simple: children identify with the good guy so that they can think of themselves as good. This enables them to project onto the bad guy their own repressed anger, violence, rebelliousness, or lust, and then vicariously to enjoy their own evil by watching the bad guy initially prevail … When the good guy finally wins, viewers are then able to reassert control over their own inner tendencies, repress them, and re-establish a sense of goodness. Salvation is guaranteed through identification with the hero … No premium is put on reasoning, persuasion, negotiation or diplomacy.[1]

The idea is that peace and order (shalom) are only established through violence. Human beings are themselves the result of a violent battle among the gods so that violence is

---

1 Wink, *Engaging the Powers*, p. 19.

in our DNA. Violence, says Wink, is the spirituality of our age, and seems simply to be the nature of things. The idea that the economy can only work through competition is an extension of this idea because with competition there will always be winners and losers. There are a whole series of 'delusional assumptions' of the domination system, among which we find:

- The need to control society and prevent chaos requires some to dominate others.
- Those who dominate may use other people as a means to achieve their goals.
- Men are better equipped by nature to be dominant than women, and some races are naturally suited to dominate others.
- A valued end justifies the use of any means.
- Ruling or managing is the most important of all social functions.
- Therefore rulers and managers should be rewarded by extra privileges and greater wealth of all kinds.
- Money is the most important value.
- The possession of money is a sign of worth.
- The production of material goods is more important than the production of healthy and normal people.
- Property is sacred and property ownership is an absolute right.

We can recognize these assumptions as foundational to our own society. Transition shares with the discipleship community a scepticism about these assumptions which Wink ascribes to 'the powers'. The powers, he says, are the 'interiority' of movements, cultures, nations and churches.

The New Testament words 'kosmos', world, 'aeon', age, and 'sarx', flesh, are various ways of speaking of the domination system. They represent society organized against God, operating according to assumptions that are contrary to God. In Wink's terms, the powers are good, fallen, and can be redeemed. The powers are good because they represent the institutional structures without which we cannot exist. They are, however, fallen. Beyond what Jung called 'the shadow' is the sedimentation of thousands of years of human choices for evil, characterized by a hellish hatred of the light, of truth, kindness and compassion. The language of the Fall is mythic language, speaking of what is constantly true. Recognition of the Fall frees us from delusions about perfectibility, which are fatal to social change movements like Transition. It make us modest about what we hope we can achieve, which allows us to be expectant towards God, and reminds us that we can only be saved from the power system by something that transcends it. But the powers can be redeemed. Jesus proclaimed the advent of the reign of God that would transform every aspect of reality, including the social framework of existence.

> The gospel is not a message of personal salvation from the world, but a message of a world transfigured, right down to its basic structures. Redemption means actually being liberated from the oppression of the Powers, being forgiven for one's own sin and of complicity with the powers, and being engaged in liberating the Powers themselves from their bondage to idolatry.[2]

---

2 Wink, *Engaging the Powers*, p. 83.

Recognition of the powers is important because there is no way we can escape their influence. As the spiritualities of movements and cultures they shape our lives to their deepest depths. Thus the spirituality of nationalism was a 'power' responsible for many of the bloodiest conflicts of the twentieth century. But in prophetic preaching, and in the life and teaching of Jesus, we find an outline of God's domination free order, which challenges all hierarchies and champions economic equality, since inequalities are the basis of domination.

The domination free order is based on the refusal to mirror violence. The Eucharist, says Wink, 'celebrates Jesus' non-violent breaking of the spiral of violence by absorbing its momentum with his own body. Jesus' way means living a life of forgiveness and doing acts of reconciliation'.[3] This is why we read in 1 Peter: 'Christ also suffered for you, leaving you an example, so that you should follow in his steps … When he was abused, he did not return abuse; when he suffered, he did not threaten.' Christ endured the cross rather than be false to his own non-violent way. If that is correct it means that there is a cruel irony in the fact that some Christian theologies have read the death of Christ as the price that has to be paid in order for sin to be forgiven, a type of theology that once more reads violence into God and makes it ultimate.

Jesus' call to the discipleship community, says Wink, is not to create a new society but to delegitimate an unjust system and create a spiritual counter-climate. This is echoed in

---

3 Wink, *Engaging the Powers*, p. 127.

the Transition idea that we have to withdraw energy from the present ruling system. At the same time there is the call to learn a third way other than fight or flight, namely non-violent direct action. Turning the other cheek is not, as many critics think, a supine acceptance of abuse. On the contrary, the blow on the right cheek is designed to humiliate and so to offer the other cheek is to refuse to be humiliated. The same goes for carrying a burden the extra mile – it is about recovering the initiative.

What the narrative of the cross says, however, is that challenging the powers is always going to be costly. Rob Hopkins thinks of a vision so attractive that people will simply want to join it. There is a great deal of emphasis on fun and celebration. Transition, this suggests, might be accomplished without pain and without conflict. Celebration is a good thing, and the insight that failure also has to be celebrated is especially valuable, but the New Testament narrative suggests that if we challenge the delusional assumptions of the powers, conflict will ensue. Conflict with the powers, and the attendant cost of discipleship, is at the heart of the New Testament. The key thing is that instead of a dualistic battle between good and evil Jesus is seeking a way in which evil can be opposed without being mirrored, finding a way that prevents us from becoming what we hate, being drawn in by the contagion of evil. Forgiveness and non-violence lie at the heart of this.

Christians should be involved in Transition because, from their perspective, it is about the establishment of shalom. The attempt, the New Testament says, will require plentiful forgiveness, not once, but over and over again. In other words, the struggle to realize a new world is something we have to commit to over and over again, which is why we have a movement, a Way.

## Questions for discussion

- If salvation is 'making whole', what are the dimensions of that in our communities?

- Where do we stand in relation to the 'delusional assumptions' of our society? Do we agree that they are delusional?

# 7

# The Long Road to Freedom

The philosopher Ludwig Wittgenstein famously taught that the meaning of a word is its use in the language. If we apply this to the word 'Spirit' as it occurs in Scripture, then we have a surprise. If you look at theology books you would assume that the word 'Spirit' occurs all the time, but it doesn't: it occurs in three great blocks. The first block is the material in Judges which records the struggle for Palestine in the tenth century BCE (the same period as Homer). Here, *ruach* (spirit) 'falls on' a whole series of men and women to lead their people and gain victory, often over superior forces. So 'spirit' is a way of talking about what it is that gives us courage and strength to overcome opposition and to gain liberation. That is assumed to come from outside people, not from their own inner resources.

What follows is especially interesting. The Philistines, probably people from the Aegean, have iron age technology but 'Israel' only has bronze age technology. A series of defeats lead Israel to adopt kingship, and under this united leadership they are able to get the upper hand. But then, in a perfect example of sociologist Max Weber's understanding of how societies work, charisma is routinized. Spirit language disappears, because it has been appropriated by the King,

and the royal ideology's claims that the Spirit works especially through him. No surprise then that the second great
band of spirit language comes after the end of the monarchy, during the 'exile'. Actually most of the people remained in Israel, but the elites were taken into captivity,
settled, and remained there until the founding of the State
of Israel. Spirit language during the 'exile' speaks of the
re-birth of the nation – it is a promise of hope to people
who feel that they might disappear into the interstices of
history, as did many of their neighbours – the Moabites,
Peruzites, Edomites and so on. Once again spirit is a way
of talking of what gives hope, what rebuilds community.
Once again it comes from outside.

One of the most interesting stories from this period is the
continuation of the passage from Numbers mentioned in
Chapter 7.

> Moshe heard the people weeping throughout their fami-
> lies, all at the entrances of their tents. Then the LORD
> became very angry, and Moshe was displeased. So
> Moshe said to the LORD, 'Why have you treated your
> servant so badly? Why have I not found favour in your
> sight, that you lay the burden of all this people on me?
> Did I conceive all this people? Did I give birth to them,
> that you should say to me, "Carry them in your bosom,
> as a nurse carries a sucking child," to the land that you
> promised on oath to their ancestors? Where am I to get
> meat to give to all this people? For they come weeping
> to me and say, "Give us meat to eat!" I am not able to
> carry all this people alone, for they are too heavy for me.
> If this is the way you are going to treat me, put me to

death at once – if I have found favour in your sight – and do not let me see my misery.'

So the LORD said to Moshe, 'Gather for me seventy of the elders of Israel, whom you know to be the elders of the people and officers over them; bring them to the tent of meeting, and have them take their place there with you. I will come down and talk with you there; and I will take some of the spirit that is on you and put it on them; and they shall bear the burden of the people along with you so that you will not bear it all by yourself.'

Given the difficulties of the journey to liberation – the transition, let us say, from oil dependency to resilience – Moshe complains to the NAME that the burden of leadership is too great for him. And who asked you to lead in that kind of way? God replies. A Transition training course is set up, and at the end of it seventy elders (i.e. a large number of people) are trained to help share the leadership. But then it turns out that two people who have not done their Transition training are also 'prophesying' – making policy proposals for the community. The trained are furious – stop them! they say to Moshe. But by now Moshe has got the message: 'Would that all the LORD's people were prophets!' In other words, the whole community is to share in running affairs. 'Spirit' falls on everyone. There are no leaders and led. It is a very Transition solution!

A century or more ago scholars began by comparing Spirit in the early books with mana, an impersonal force; they then traced the 'ethicization' of the idea in the great prophets, and ended in the post-exilic literature identifying the Spirit with God. This way of understanding spirit rested on an overestimate of the importance of the root meaning of *ruach* or *pneuma* as wind or breath and a pre-occupation with religion as something inward and spiritual. In fact, our texts suggest something different. The connection of the Spirit with politics, history, rule and order is overwhelming. The primary context is justice and a new society.

The third great band of spirit material is in the messianic writings – the writings witnessing to Jesus the *maschiach* (usually called, in the light of Jeremiah 31, the 'New Testament'). In the gospels the primary reference of spirit language is messianic, with clear connotations of judgement, and the establishment of a new order. Luke in particular regards petitionary prayer as the means by which the power of God's Spirit becomes real in history. Spirit, kingdom and prayer go together. For John, Jesus is the bearer and bestower of the Spirit, through which the work he began during his ministry, and which was accomplished on the cross, is carried on into the future.

The person who is most responsible for the use of spirit language in the church, however, is Paul, who uses it more than a hundred times. Whether there was an event of 'Pentecost' as Luke describes it or not, 'something must have happened' to account for this intensity of reference (to use Transition terminology, Pentecost was 'the great unleashing'). Some powerfully experienced reality lies behind this. Paul's horizon is the overcoming of the division between Jews and Gentiles, which for him is a foretaste of the breaking down of all barriers and the inauguration of a new creation. 'Spirit' is the name for what makes this possible. The Spirit builds up the church, bestows gifts, and wars against the flesh ('flesh' here is not the body, and not sexuality – a common mistake. It is all things that characterize a non-kingdom centred life – preoccupation with 'stuff', privilege, money and so forth). I note that Jesus put the rule of God at the heart of his teaching. For Paul Jesus instantiates that rule, and 'Spirit' is what makes the order he instantiates a presently realized reality. For him humanity stands at the threshold of a new order. The word 'spiritual' does not describe a higher aspect of human life, and especially not religious life. It means that the Spirit of God renewing creation is at work in human society and in each person. Paul presupposes the story in Numbers 11: every Christian has the Spirit, and that recognition must not be quenched.

To some extent it might be said that the same thing happened to spirit language under the church as happened during the monarchy – the church tried to take it over, and insist that outside it there was no spirit, that it controlled what could be said was of the Spirit and what was not. In this respect the history of all the fringe movements in Christian history – up to the present – is fascinating. One could view Christian history as an attempt to keep the lid on all the energies and creativity of the new movement that were attributed to the Spirit – the reality and generative capacity – of Jesus. This has always proved impossible. Beginning with the Montanists in the second century, right through the Brethren of the free Spirit in medieval Europe, the Anabaptists of the sixteenth century, the Ranters, Levellers, Diggers and Quakers of the seventeenth century and the Pentecostalists of the nineteenth and twentieth centuries the movement has always been impossible to contain. The historian of many of these movements, Norman Cohn, spoke of 'the messianism of the disoriented poor'. That does not apply to quite all of these movements, or to all forms of Pentecostalism today, but what we can say is that to use spirit language is to see the creativity of the end and origin of all things, the NAME, at work in human life and society in all those movements that seek the *melkuth YHWH*, the situation of shalom, both between humans but also between human beings and the non-human world. In that respect it is not so surprising that the Transition might be described as 'a great movement of the Spirit'. What Christians involved in Transition will want to add to the practical community building work is what Ched Myers calls biblical and critical literacy: learning to use Scripture as 'the fundamental interpretive code ... to delegitimize discourses of domination and legitimize radical practice'.[1] This will be at the heart of their own understanding of inner Transition, of what it is that inspires and guides us on the long road to freedom, to a society of shalom.

## Questions for discussion

- What are the discourses of domination – inside and outside the church – which we need to delegitimize?
- Where might we discern the Spirit in our own times?

---

1 Myers, *Who Will Roll Away the Stone?*, p. 71.

# 8

# Praise

'The philosophers have only interpreted the world: the point however is to change it': the best summary ever written of John's Gospel. The Digger Gerrard Winstanley's watchword, 'In action is the life of man', is a genuinely biblical motto. But at the same time *ekklesia* is not just activism. At the heart of everything it does is something else – worship. Worship – including the most formal, a Bach motet for example – is ecstatic. That is to say, it is about being centred outside yourself and your own concerns. The claim is that precisely this is liberating. The psalms of the Hebrew bible are full of praise. Psalm 29 says:

> Ascribe to YHWH, O heavenly beings,
> Ascribe to YHWH glory and strength.
> Ascribe to YHWH the glory of God's name;
> Worship YHWH in the sacred court. (vv 1–2)

Praise, says Walter Wink, is the homoestatic principle of the universe. 'It preserves the harmony of the whole by preventing usurpation of the whole by its parts. Praise is the ecological principle of divinity whereby every creature is subordinated to its organic relationship with the Creator. Praise is the cure for the apostasy of the Powers.'[1]

---

1 Wink, *Engaging the Powers*, p. 167.

Praise is not a specifically religious phenomenon: we praise people, and hear them praised, all the time and this teaches us to be wary. Shakespeare offers us a wry take on the false praise we call flattery in Sonnet 130:

> My mistress' eyes are nothing like the sun;
> Coral is far more red than her lips' red;
> If snow be white, why then her breasts are dun;
> If hairs be wires, black wires grow on her head ...
> I grant I never saw a goddess go;
> My mistress when she walks treads on the ground.
> > And yet, by heaven, I think my love as rare
> > As any she belied with false compare.

Having disposed of all the empty hyperboles that constitute so much praise he comes back to the reality, the 'recognition, respect and delight' which theologians Dan Hardy and David Ford find at the heart of praise. Praise, they say, perfects perfection – it adds something, enhances what is already valued.[2] Think of the moment at the end of a concert, or of a play, when the audience erupts in applause. This goes beyond convention and there are occasions when it is especially moving. The rapturous applause for Daniel Barenboim's East-West orchestra, which brings Arabs and Israelis together to play, or the Venezuelan or Soweto Youth Orchestras, goes beyond the music, recognizing the power of the music to transcend poverty, alienation and hatred. Indeed, those experiences inform the music. What moves us to get to our feet on these occasions? It is an act

---

2 Dan Hardy and David Ford, *Jubilate: Theology in Praise*, London: Darton, Longman and Todd, 1984, p. 6.

of generosity of spirit, called out from us and then given back to us. This stepping outside ourselves, existing for a moment purely in the delight of some transcendent other or experience, is one of the key aspects of our humanness. This delight in that which is not ourselves is at the heart of worship. Augustine begins his Confessions by arguing that human beings are born with an inbuilt drive to praise God:

> You are great, O Lord, and greatly to be praised; your power is great, and your wisdom infinite. Human beings are your creatures and want to praise you. They carry the mark of death, the sign of sin, to remind them that you 'thwart the proud' but still, this tiny part of your creation wants to praise you. You have created them in such a way that they delight to praise you, for you have made us for yourself and our hearts are restless until they find their rest in you.

Thanksgiving is at the heart of it. 'I can no other answer make but thanks, and thanks, and ever thanks,' says Sebastian to Antonio in *Twelfth Night*. Thanks is the response to the self-gifting of the NAME which is free and for nothing, and which establishes all reality in the first place. The understanding that our whole life is given to be praise to the NAME has always lain at the heart of Christian life, taking very various forms in the Orthodox liturgy, in the Benedictine round of work and prayer, and in Protestant psalm and hymn singing. To give thanks is to take pleasure in God, a pleasure that gives us back to ourselves newly made. In its purest and most absolute form it is adoration – the response of love and thanksgiving to the one whose love is perfect. For many people this is most easily expressed in singing, something we do with others, and in which our bodies and souls are equally involved.

The main act of worship in most churches (though not all) is the Eucharist, a word that comes from the Greek verb *eucharisteo*, to give thanks. At the heart of it whoever presides gives thanks for what the NAME has done, above all for what occurred in Jesus of Nazareth, for his death and resurrection. What happens here is what John's Gospel speaks of as a sign, a sign that praise and adoration of the source and end of all things takes place everywhere – just as the Benedicite reminds us. The Eucharist is part of, and a sign to remind us of, that praise. It reminds us of the limitlessness of the divine self-gifting. Crucially it precisely does not set up a marker between 'sacred' and secular': some experiences and places that are holy and others that are not. No one has written of this better than the Jesuit theologian Karl Rahner:

> The world and its history are the terrible and sublime liturgy, breathing of death and sacrifice, which God celebrates and causes to be celebrated in and through human history in its freedom, this being something which he in turn sustains in grace by his sovereign disposition. In the entire length and breadth of this immense history of birth and death, complete superficiality and folly, inadequacy and hatred (all of which 'crucify') on the one hand, and silent submission, responsibility even to death in dying and in joyfulness, in attaining the heights and plumbing the depths, on the other, the liturgy of the world is present ... [This liturgy] must be interpreted and 'reflected upon' in its ultimate depths in the celebration of that

which we are accustomed to call liturgy in the most usual sense. But this second liturgy must draw from the liturgy of the world ... The Mass is a sign in miniature of the mass of the world, to which obviously Christ himself belongs.[3]

The praise of the Eucharist takes a narrative form. The worshipper is incorporated into the story, becomes part of it, its latest chapter, as that story forms their life, centring it on the ecstatic self-gifting of God and calling each one into the life of the 'rule of God'.

The praise of the Eucharist includes, puzzlingly for non-Christians, an act of penance. An atheist colleague commented that while she could appreciate most of a church service she found this part demeaning. In fact precisely this is liberating, because it is a way of dealing with the constant tendency to foul up, to make a mess of our lives, and therefore of the lives of others, to find forgiveness and therefore the possibility of starting again – of Transition. Confession of sin and forgiveness, followed by praise, is also a very different thing from the therapy referred to in Rob Hopkins' *The Transition Companion*. Though healing is part of salvation, what is understood here is a liberation that flows from the source of all life, known in community and practised within a particular tradition, and not a possibility intrinsic to the psyche.

In Transition, celebration and thanksgiving serves a similar purpose and is part and parcel of community activity.

3 Karl Rahner, *Theological Investigations*, Vol. 14, London: Darton, Longman and Todd, 1976, p. 169.

Sharing food convivially is a way of drawing people together. It is a gift that brings great joy and builds community coherence. Transition also urges that groups should celebrate and acknowledge failure. For Christians worship and praise are always going to be at the heart of any process of social transformation, without which the process runs the danger of becoming introverted and shallow. Praise, it turns out, is not an optional extra, but a key part of the movement of liberation.

## Questions for discussion

- How does praise inform our everyday lives?

- What might be its impact for our understanding of the economy?

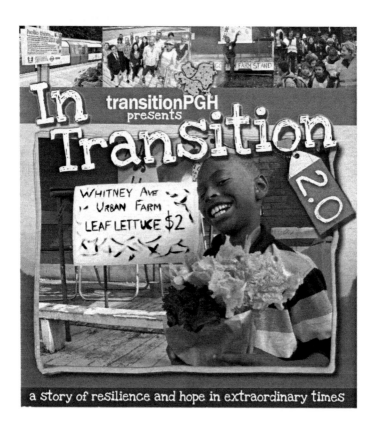

transitionPGH
presents

In Transition 2.0

WHITNEY AVE
URBAN FARM
LEAF LETTUCE $2

a story of resilience and hope in extraordinary times

# 9

# Hope and Despair

Many thousands of people are involved in Transition but politicians still talk about endless growth, and where they have money people still seem guided by hedonism. Climate scientists warn that the task of addressing climate change is immensely urgent, but many world leaders, including those in the UK, did not even bother to turn up to Rio+20 (UN Conference on Sustainable Development 2012). Peak oil analysts increasingly warn about runaway oil prices, but so far no steps to ration oil are in place: people still behave as if it will last for ever. Is it realistic to hope for a saner future? Is hope legitimate, or does it delude us? Does it encourage us to believe in never-never land, u-topia (no-place)?

The question is about the ground of hope. Since the eighteenth century, at least, the ground of hope has been in human ability, in the promise of technology. One can quite see why: the technological and medical progress of the past 250 years has been extraordinary, but as we know to our cost it has a very dark downside. This progress has also brought us nuclear weapons and other increasingly efficient ways of killing people, and now, according to many scientists, could threaten the very existence of life on earth. Technology, it seems, has not been guided by wisdom. The ecological crisis, Jürgen Moltmann notes, is not just a moral crisis but a religious crisis of the paradigm in which people in the Western world put their trust and live. Can this crisis be resolved?

It certainly cannot be resolved by the 'realism' to which politicians of all shades still appeal. In the 2010 election in Great Britain the then Prime Minister, Gordon Brown, dismissed an opponent who wanted to get rid of Britain's nuclear defences on the grounds that this was not practical politics. One wonders what he meant by 'practical'. The same 'realism' currently determines policies about growth, economics and climate change, as well as about defence. This 'realism' will destroy us.

Over against this realism is a realism of a firmly grounded hope. For Paul the NAME, the God of exodus and resurrection, is the ground of hope. In Scripture the book that reflects this is the book of Revelation, the happy hunting ground for fundamentalists, cranks and futurologists of all kinds. In fact it is underground literature which is addressed to those who are hoping against hope in bleak and often desperate situations. The author speaks of an angel mixing incense to mingle with the prayers of believers.

> When the Lamb opened the seventh seal, there was silence in heaven for about half an hour. Then I saw the seven angels who stand before God, and seven trumpets were given to them. And another angel came and stood at the altar with a golden censer; and he was given much incense to mingle with the prayers of all the saints upon the golden altar before the throne.

The smoke of the incense is a counterweight to the cloud full of evil that rises from the bottomless pit and the smoke that rises from the burning city of Babylon/Rome (18.9–18). Is there a connection? Could it be, asks the Dutch scholar Bas Wielenga, that the prayers of the saints may have an explosive effect? Could it be that empires fall because powerless people keep up the prayer for God's kingdom to come? This is a message to those concerned about rising sea-levels, and pollution of the earth and sea and rivers. It is both a call to repentance, which means to change lifestyles, and also a message of hope.

Hope is grounded in Scripture by the fact that God keeps God's promises and that these are paradigmatically manifested in the resurrection of the crucified. 'The crucifixion and resurrection of Jesus are the assurance that there is a force at work in the world to transform even the most crushing defeat into divine victory. We are thus freed from having to succeed; we have only to be faithful ... We are freed from despair; we have only to trust the One in and through whom and for whom all things exist.'[1] This means in the first place that the radically new is possible in the midst of history. In the light of the resurrection it is no longer possible to say that history runs on iron laws, that it is only possible to expect what our theories and axioms allow. Faith in the resurrection is the ground on which Christians hope for a *different* future, a transition to a society less destructive, more peaceful and more whole. Living in this hope grounds the Christian ethic of resistance and calls *ekklesia* to live as a 'contrast community' to society.

---

1 Wink, *Engaging the Powers*, p., 219.

In his language of new creation Paul also addresses what today we call the second law of thermodynamics. Of course all created reality will perish but, says Paul, it was created by the NAME and will return to the NAME. God is life in Godself and the future of all created things is in God's inexhaustible life. Death is 'the last enemy', which still has to be overcome. This does not mean that the present ceases to be important, because all reality comes from and is held by the One who wills life.

But secondly, the frustration and failures we experience in dealing with climate change are those that every generation experiences. This is why it matters that we are dealing with the resurrection of the *crucified*. This means that these failures are, as Jürgen Moltmann says, 'taken up into the confidence of hope, while on the other hand hope's confidence becomes earthly and universal'.

To say that we are called to hope does not mean that we believe in history's happy end. Writing as someone who, as a 16 year old, manned anti-aircraft guns as Hamburg was firebombed and reduced to rubble, and who was then drafted into Hitler's desperate armies, captured, and spent four years as a POW, Moltmann goes on:

> In the present situation of our world, facile consolation is as fatal as melancholy hopelessness. No one can assure us that the worst will not happen. According to the laws of experience it will. We can only trust that even the end of the world hides a new beginning if we trust the God who calls into being the things that are not, and out of death creates new life. Life out of this hope then means

already acting here and today in accordance with that world of justice and righteousness and peace, contrary to appearances, and contrary to all historical chances of success. It obliges us solemnly to abjure the spirit, logic and practice of the nuclear system of deterrence and all other systems of mass annihilation. It means an unconditional Yes to life in the face of the inescapable death of all the living.[2]

That unconditional Yes is what motivates Christians to be involved in Transition. The discipleship community is not asked to go it alone, or to reinvent the wheel. It is asked to get involved in a project which in many ways echoes its own deepest convictions and intuitions in creating a future that is more just and certainly more sustainable than the present. Many initiatives are already in place – like the eco-congregation programme. But these remain church centred. Christians are part of civil society and as such they get involved in political parties, trades unions, non-governmental organizations and so forth. By becoming a Transition church, Christians can partner with other groups in their town or city, engaging with energy, food and inner Transition. The training that Transition provides can help the discipleship community to learn more about resilience and the strength of working together and this community will gain access to the myriad resources that can help bolster attempts at greening our world, and nurturing our communities back to health.

---

2 Jürgen Moltmann, *The Coming of God*, London: SCM Press, 1996, p. 235.

It seems to us that the potential to help one another is great. Transition's inspirational message (that the transition from oil dependency to resilient local communities is possible and can be achieved by ordinary people working together) helps flesh out the church's understanding of the human role in serving creation and realizing God's will on earth, and gives renewed hope. This book is a call to the discipleship community to get involved – urgently – in the task of Transition.

# Resources

## For Transition

### Books all published by Green Books, Dartington

Carolyn Baker, *Navigating the Coming Chaos: A Handbook for Inner Transition*, 2011.

Chris Bird, *Local Sustainable Homes: How to Make them Happen*, 2010.

Shaun Chamberlain, *The Transition Timeline*, 2009.

Rob Hopkins, *The Transition Companion: Making Your Community More Resilient in Uncertain Times*, 2011.

Rob Hopkins, *The Transition Handbook: From Oil Dependency to Local Resilience*, 2008.

Tamzin Pinkerton and Rob Hopkins, *Local Food and How to Make it Happen*, 2009.

Alexis Rowell, *Communities, Councils and a Low Carbon Future*, 2010.

### Website

www.transitionnetwork.org
Many local groups have their own very effective websites – always worth checking.

## For Churches

Wendell Berry, *Home Economics: Fourteen Essays*, San Francisco: North Point, 1987; Counterpoint, 2009.

Wendell Berry, *What Matters? Economics for a Renewed Commonwealth*, Berkeley: Counterpoint, 2010.

Herman Daly and John Cobb, *For the Common Good*, Boston: Beacon Press, 1989.

Ulrich Duchrow and Franz Hinkelammert, *Transcending Greedy Money*, London: Palgrave Macmillan, 2012.

Dan Hardy and David Ford, *Jubilate: Theology in Praise*, London: Darton, Longman and Todd, 1984.

Jürgen Moltmann, *God in Creation*, London: SCM Press, 1984.

Jürgen Moltmann, *The Coming of God*, London: SCM Press, 1996.

Ched Myers, *Binding the Strong Man*, Maryknoll: Orbis, 1988.

Ched Myers, *Who Will Roll Away the Stone?: Discipleship Queries for First World Christians*, Maryknoll: Orbis, 1994.

Michael Northcott, *A Moral Climate: The Ethics of Global Warming*, London: Darton, Longman and Todd; New York: Orbis Books, 2007.

Walter Wink, *Engaging the Powers*, Minneapolis: Fortress, 1992.

## Websites

www.christian-ecology.org.uk
www.operationnoah.org
www.justice-and-peace.org.uk
www.ecocongregation.org